Loving who you are
where you are

Loving who you are where you are

theta burke

Delafield Press   Suttons Bay, Michigan 49682

ISBN: 0-916872-07-6
Library of Congress Catalog Card Number: 82-71079
Printed in the United States of America

I see you in a special way
the way I think
        your soul would say.

Loving who you are where you are

through the searching

speaking and reaching

toward integrity

through the searching

1.

Early needs
unmet
leave spaces of hurt
but they also speak Awareness
And the pain of their absence
becomes the sand that irritates
to cause the pearl.

2.

There's a lonely part
way down inside
that doesn't go away
a hidden part
that cries alone
that I can never say.
A part of me feels missing
that I can't seem to find—
a soul in pain
seems all there is
Will ever peace be mine?

3.

Through the inside dark
will you walk with me
will you stay — not leave me alone
will you feel the anguish that lives inside
will you come with me — can you really know?

                    Perhaps if you
                    can view with me
                    those parts of me
                    I fear to see
                    I'll come to let
                    those parts exist
                    let them be
                    and not resist

the pain I've felt
and tried to hide
keeping parts of me outside.

4.

Scattered bits
and scattered pieces
that's the way life seems to me
can't see a way
to get together
all the things I'd like to be.

Spinning wheels
in all directions
that's the way life seems to be
no foundation
standing solid
that's the way it feels to me.

Bits and pieces
bits and pieces
scattered much too far to reach
just can't get
them all together
scattered bits of what is me

Help me find a way to see
help me put together me.

5.

When I'm lost and alone
if my soul has no home
my journey cannot lead inside
there's a place yet to go
a way I need know
before I can see what's inside.

My heart must feel
from another
a love to ignite my own
who will love what he sees
in the way I can be
it's then that my soul can come home.

6.

With no love to feel
I've no love to give
and life's just one big charade
oh, I've learned my part well
I have stories to tell
just listen — and watch me on stage.

But the curtain falls
and I'm empty
of whatever it is I may seem
I cannot speak love
until I feel love
and how does this love come to be?

Yet the emptiness
makes me keep searching
for the *something* that I've never known
and if I want to see
perhaps it can be
then love to my heart will be known.

7.

How can one
who has always heard
      Love's message
feel the pain of the emptiness
in one to whom
it has only whispered.

8.

Somewhere
in some yesterday
a soul touched my own
so that I became aware
     of Love.

All loneliness
and all yearning
is for the fullness
     of what was awakened
All joy is the expression
of what was known
and all pain its absence.

My journey
to that completion
is my Reason.

speaking and reaching

9.

When I fear to speak
the truth of me to others
I am afraid
      they will not accept me.

When I cannot speak it
      to myself
I have not accepted me.

10.

Those times when I can feel no hope
I need to know that my hopelessness
        is accepted.
The times when I am unable to do
those things I would like,
know how much I want to
And just be there.
I feel more discouraged with me
than you possibly could.

I want a Way
but I cannot yet see one
You say I should search.
I have — and I am.
The searchings may not be visible to you
but the inside strength is spent
              over and over again
And when the outside may appear untroubled,
often the pain is being covered over.
I reach a point beyond the spending
              and only exist.

Don't *ask* me to reach.
I do it all the time.

11.

Our answers
are a part of our questions.
Some questions
we are ready to speak aloud,
some we keep within.
But in whatever manner we ask
our journey to the answer
       has begun.

12.

Love
once felt
will never leave you.
Its faces may change
and its presence may be
        at times o'ershadowed
but it is an Essence
more real than your heartbeat.

Do not ascribe or limit
        its existence
to a mutual affection.

13.

With a heavy heart
and a tortured soul
she goes along her way
doing what
she has to do
just getting through the day.

Her strength is tried
she longs for rest
somewhere to lay the burden down
it bends her low
and her soul cries out
When can I lay me down?

> There seems no way
> for me to go
> to do the things I must
> the love I felt
> has gone away
> how can I ever trust?

But I see her travel onward
through a haze she cannot see
for the love she's felt
has made her grow
beyond what she can see.

And though the flame
may flicker low
I know that it won't die
the love that's causing
all the pain
will lead to reasons why

Reasons why
beyond what's seen
that guide her soul along
when light is dim
and faith seems gone
Love leaves not the soul alone.

14.

A whitened fist
all tight with rage
speaking the anger hidden away
trying to find a way to be
afraid to let another see.

How will I speak of what I feel
I'm afraid of what's within
so long the anger has bound me
where do I begin?

I fear to be lest I lose control
and destroy what I have
and yet I know for standing strong
I need to be what's felt
       admit the anger hidden there
       learning love and pain to share.

15.

Our vulnerability
may seem to be decreased
        by emotional distance
But that only increases
the alienation.

16.

Concrete actions
or promises
can never insure
      relationships.

Only a spiritual affinity
allows this.

17.

You get a cold
it's not your fault
it's something you have "caught"
and a broken leg
is there to see
you're not blamed — it's not your fault.

Emotions are seen
a different way
they say it's up to you
to do the things
that make you whole
and you should choose a better view.

Can thinking heal
a broken leg
or calm a tortured mind
I think that you'd
agree with me
if I said they both take time

     but the one is blamed
     and the other's not
     for the kind of misery he's got.

So the pain that comes
from deep inside
which can't be seen
feels a need to hide
because so many cannot see
and think that you just *let* it be

      So much better it would be
      if only they could really see
      and understand what I can't help
      I think I'd feel a better self

not having pain *and* blame to bear
as I try to manage what is there.

18.

From inner battle he has come.
The wounds from the struggle
        do not show
but the weariness
lies deep in his soul.

Time
will speak its healing
and many will forget
But he will know
        the scars.

19.

All the stories never told
all the sadness in his soul
pain too close
to share in words

      Help him know
      his soul is heard.

20.

Within you
lie the answers
to all you would seek.

Time and love
and adherence to your truth
will cause their speaking.

21.

If the wall of your anger
will not allow my entering
          the arena of discussion
how will our differences
be understood
          and resolved?

22.

Misunderstandings
unresolved
feed the coffers
of defensiveness and hostility
and make increasingly difficult
        accurate communication.

23.

One never *intends*
to be selfish.
His actions
speak only his need
and his learning
        of Love.

24.

So often
she seemed to speak too quickly
of others' shortcomings.

But then
I had to remember
her impatience
      with her own.

25.

He who had seemed
      to seek battle
stood now with no adversary
And he came to know
his foe had been himself.

26.

Because things inside
felt so tenuous and uncertain
she used much of the power
          of her intellect
to assure the certainty
of external affairs.

Some didn't understand
and called her
          a Manipulator.

27.

How quickly
the fire of joy
    is doused
by self-condemnation.

28.

She tried to do
just as they'd say
be very, very good
and never tried to do a thing
they didn't think she should
      when she was small.

And later on
her years in school
were efforts for good grades
to please the teachers was her aim
her need was for their praise.

And then she aimed
to please her husband
be a very good wife indeed
never thinking to look inside
to hear what her soul would speak

Now on and on
through life she goes
doing what she "should"
while starving that which is her soul
not knowing *her own should.*

29.

Pain
physical or emotional
takes a heavy toll
      on our energy level.

Patience
with its healing
      in ourselves or others
is its request.

30.

Some would say
we are responsible
      for what we feel.
I would say, rather,
that our responsibility lies
in how we *act*
      upon our feelings.

And accepting what they are
does not necessarily imply
that we should follow
      their impulse.

31.

Your love
was strong enough
to provide the bridge
        from you to myself.

Now I can walk
        back and forth
and help others
build bridges.

32.

One reached out
in her need
and found a response.

Another there was
whose need was even greater
but she was unable to reach
because she felt too uncertain
of how to handle
      the response.

33.

When a spider *begins*
to spin his web,
how does he get from here to there?
The materials he needs
are all inside—
he doesn't spin his web from air.

34.

She affirmed herself
     by meeting others' needs
and could not believe herself essential
when no tasks were to be done.

35.

If I ask of you
what I would give,
to me it's a proper request
But if you refuse
because you choose
then I let your decision rest.

36.

Ideal soil
makes for shallow roots.
In rocky or sandy soil
the roots must reach deep
      for nourishment
and for firm anchorage
against the elements.

Experience is our soil.

37.

When the fire is low
some shifting of the logs
can make it burn
        more effectively.

Adjusting our attitudes
often does the same
        for our lives.

38.

Long years ago
when but a lad
the love of his life was killed
and now when death
takes someone dear
he strikes out as to kill.

> Why does he try
> to hurt, ask they,
> attempting to have
> things go *his* way?

His anger speaks
to those he loves
in ways they do not understand.
Does the hurt and rage
that a boy once felt
still live in the heart of a man?

39.

Love sees
      cares
      hopes
      believes
      endures
      is patient
      forgives
and seeks to understand.

Loving who you are
where you are
allows the freedom to choose
and unbinds the energy
      to become more.

40.

As you give what you need
in the measure you can
it becomes the magnet
        for attracting more
unto yourself.

toward integrity

41.

I am
(not because I do)

I do
(because I am)

42.

We are each
a piece of a great puzzle.
How can I contribute
        to its working, then,
if I attempt to borrow
your form or character?

43.

A moment of high excitement
is that time in a man's life
when the inward voice
       directs his course
and he feels the freedom
of himself.

44.

When I am not
what I would be
I cheat myself
and injure thee.
I need not hear
words of reproof
     (my soul speaks those)
speak thou, my love,
some words to soothe.

45.

When one acts toward another
a way he would not choose
        to experience,
he pushes himself farther
from the shore of his Truth.

46.

Speak not to others
all your hopes and fears
or successes and failures.

Keep always within
      something of that
known only to thee
as soil wherein may grow
new seeds of Self
      lying protected
from the praise or doubts
of others.

47.

When the soul reaches the level
of exhaustion
which causes it to speak *I can't,*
perhaps that is its reply
      to others' expectations
and may indeed be the beginning
of the soul's realization
      of its own autonomy.

48.

I am truly vulnerable
only to that
        which I have not accepted
about myself.

49.

To resist one's Self
to push away from what one *is*
is alienation.
And great energy is required
to maintain this separation.

Communication and alliance
with the soul
      is the way to peace.

50.

Fidelity to one's soul
in its flux
requires great faith
in that soul's knowledge
     which questions not
its direction.

51.

The pains of life and love
should not be denied
        or cast aside.
Accept the wounds of your soul
and let the scars become reminders
        to your understanding
of the hurts of others.

52.

Is it possible
for one to come unto
      the truth of himself
without drawing upon
a greater Truth
of which he is a part?

53.

We cling to
and espouse a creed
spoken by others
until we feel the freedom
     to live our own.

54.

He died
shoveling snow.
And they said of him
He should not have been doing that.

But does not a man
have to do
what he feels he must?

Would doing less
      be living?

55.

One attuned to the spirit
which speaks from deep within
hears a truer gospel
than ever from other men.

56.

We make heroes of some
because we need those
    who have spoken
our higher nature.

Would that we aspire
to walk in the light
    of our own soul's truth
and we would all be heroes.

57.

Freedom
is the coming of one
        unto himself
with an awareness and acceptance
of his humanity
and a confidence
        in his divinity.

58.

Treasures and pains
of experiences and insights
        are your gifts.
Speak these
in all the moods
that are you
with the sensitivity that reveals
        the depths of each
and mutes the harshness
of the pain.